My Travels With Amy

by

Mario D. Bartoletti

Illustrations by Lili Bartoletti
Cover photo by Guillermo Perez

Order this book online at www.trafford.com
or email orders@trafford.com

Most Trafford titles are also available at major online book retailers.

Note for Librarians: A cataloguing record for this book is available from Library
and Archives Canada at www.collectionscanada.ca/amicus/index-e.html

Printed in Victoria, BC, Canada.

ISBN: 978-1-4251-6760-8 (sc)

*Our mission is to efficiently provide the world's finest, most comprehensive book publishing
service, enabling every author to experience success. To find out how to publish your book, your
way, and have it available worldwide, visit us online at www.trafford.com*

Trafford rev. 8/18/2009

www.trafford.com

North America & international
toll-free: 1 888 232 4444 (USA & Canada)
phone: 250 383 6864 ♦ fax: 812 355 4082

INTRODUCTION

Traveling with any youngster is always something of an adventure. With my three year old granddaughter Amy, it was a series of surprises and misadventures which delighted her and often startled me.

The wonderful thing about being a grandfather is the *déja vu* experience of it all. The delightful little creature trotting along beside me brought back a myriad of memories of her Mom at that age. But such awareness is bitter-sweet for most grandparents; this may be our last opportunity to see children in the family growing up. That awareness adds a special zest which for me was three parts their young age, three parts nostalgia, and four parts gratitude. The gratitude was for the opportunity to be once again a meaningful part of a child's life.

Amy is one of five grandchildren, all equally dear, yet each precious in his or her own unique way. As circumstances developed, it was little Amy who happened to travel with me several times on trips from Toronto to Florida where my wife Lili recently had opened an affiliate office for our firm. Amy had always been very close to her Grammy, who was now living in the Tampa area where she managed the new operation. Accompanying Pappi on a few business trips seemed a logical way for Amy to occasionally visit her. As it turned out, those travels were to bring Amy closer to me as well as to her Grammy.

Our travels, described here, occurred in 1989 and 1990 when Amy was three and a half to four years of age. My hope is that these anecdotal vignettes and illustrations will evoke similar memories for other grandparents.

CHAPTER I

Amy's First Flight: How Thrilling!

Amy's first flight was very exciting for her and a lot of fun for me. Watching her rising anticipation those weeks before the trip was a fascinating experience. Well before our departure, Amy had packed her little round Barbie travel-case with the best of her underwear, socks, PJs and her swimsuit - as well as several blouses and shorts. Of course, some of those items needed to be worn during the week. So, after her mother had washed them, Amy would fret until she actually got the clean items back from the laundry. Then, she would meticulously re-pack her suitcase. No one could accuse Amy of not being ready on time!

When the big day arrived, Amy was literally "hot to trot"! On the way to the airport, her tongue never stopped; she commented on everything and everybody. "That car is going too fast! It isn't very sunny today. How far is the airport?" As we drove up to the Toronto Terminal, her flashing brown eyes caught sight of a large plane taxiing on the tarmac. "Look, Pappi! Look at that plane! Isn't that thrilling?"

But the excitement Amy felt seeing that plane was nothing compared to her exuberance just forty-five minutes later as we actually boarded the flight to Pittsburgh, the first leg of our journey to Tampa.

"Here's the airplane, Amy. We're going aboard."

"The airplane! The airplane! This is so thrilling!"

Once inside the plane, she walked jauntily up the aisle. I leaned over and tapped her shoulder. "Okay, sweetheart," I said, "Here are our seats. You can sit by the window."

I placed Amy's travel case and my briefcase in the overhead compartment; she crawled up on the seat. Settling back on her folded legs, she stared at the busy world of the airport which lay beyond the window.

"Look, Pappi. Look over there! There's a great big airplane!"

"Yes, Amy. I see it! It really *is* a big plane."

"Yes. It's a *really big* plane. Is this a big plane, too?"

"Yes. This is a big plane, too."

"Oh, Pappi: This is so thrilling!" She had obviously learned a new word recently, and was using it at every opportunity.

As the flight attendants moved up and down the aisle preparatory to take-off, I helped Amy to buckle in. She waved to a stewardess, who smiled and wished her a "fun flight". One look at Amy's face left little doubt that a fun flight was exactly what she had in mind.

Slowly, the plane began to move. The tractor at the nose wheel was pushing our plane away from the boarding ramp. Amy was facing the window, a stream of words tumbling out of her mouth.

"The plane is going backwards! Now, it's stopped! Why is it stopped, Pappi? Oh, now the plane is going forwards. Where is it going? Are the other planes going to stay here? There's another plane; it's moving too! Will it bump into us?"

Amy's excited commentary continued unabated as our plane taxied into position on the runway for take-off.

"Okay, Amy. The plane is going to take off, now."

"Pappi! We're going so fast!"

Settling back on her folded legs

"Yes. Look at the ground. We're going to take off. Here we go-o-o!"

"We're getting higher and higher, Pappi. It's really thrilling!"

"Look, Amy," I said, after unbuckling. "See all the little cars? And there's a train, too."

"Yes Pappi, yes. I see them. They're so little. We're really up high."

Within a few minutes, our plane had climbed above the clouds and was rapidly gaining altitude. Amy, her face still pressed against the window, looked perplexed.

"Where *is* everything, Pappi?" I can't see the little cars and the train!"

"Those are clouds, sweetheart. We're way above the clouds, now."

Amy looked down at the grayish-white mass which so abruptly had cut off her view. Her ebullient mood was clearly over.

"Well", she said matter-of-factly, "The thrilling is all gone!"

By the time we reached Pittsburgh, Amy was a seasoned flyer. She had enjoyed her croissant and orange juice. "Can I have another one?" she asked.

She soon tried out the washroom. "It's too tight in here!"

She had also colored several pictures in her coloring book. "I need more crayons!"

As we got off the plane for our transfer, Amy's right hand clenched the handle of her travel case. In her hurry to run out the door, she didn't hear the stewardess. "Hope you had a fun flight, darling!"

"She did," I assured the young lady, as I rushed out to keep up with my gallivanting granddaughter. "After one flight, she's a veteran!"

The Pittsburgh terminal offered an endless series of diversions for Amy. She was eager to try a hot fudge sundae, and much to my surprise, she finished it. Any attempt to help her with anything was met with a firm statement: "I can do it *myself!*" That applied to cleaning her fudge-stained lips, replacing the sneaker which had fallen off her left foot, and opening the bag of peanuts she wanted to eat.

"I can *do* it, Pappi!" Her self-confidence was exceeded only by her tenacity. With one task after another, Amy had demonstrated a combination of competence and commitment. Only rarely was she prepared to acknowledge to an adult any absence of personal ability. Most often she would apply herself diligently, the tip of her tongue protruding between her teeth. More likely than not, she would successfully complete each task that came her way. By the time we reached Tampa, her litany of knowledge and achievement had reached Olympian heights.

"I can wash my own hands! I'll put on my own shoes! I can hold my own glass!"

Amy's independence was remarkable for a three-year-old. So, it came as no surprise to me what happened after her joyous reunion with her grandmother. As we walked out of the Tampa terminal and across the parking garage, her grandmother reached out. "Here, Amy. Take Grammy's hand."

"I'll take my *own* hand!" Amy replied resolutely. She clasped her hands together around the handle of her travel case and walked vigorously ahead of us towards Grammy's white convertible.

"I'll take my own hand!" Amy replied resolutely.

CHAPTER II

A Show of Independence

An early addition to Amy's vocabulary when she was about two years old was her exuberant expression: "We go! We go!" Whether she was leaving with her Mommy for a short trip to the market or watching her new electric train whirl its way around the figure eight track, her usual reaction to any form of motion was usually the same: "We go! We go!"

By the time she was 2 ½ years old, Amy had begun to lose some of the expressions which the family had associated with those early months when she first began to talk. Her mind was agile. Her grasp of new words and expressions was rapid. Grammy and Pappi may have mourned the loss of Amy's unique baby talk, but Amy herself had little time (and even less interest) in preserving such relics of her babyhood. She was soaking up a new and expanding vocabulary from television, overheard conversations, and goodness only knows what other sources.

For example, on the return flight of that first trip together, we had a brief layover in Philadelphia. Amy informed me that she had to use the washroom "very quickly". I immediately took her to the nearest men's room. Placing myself between Amy and the row of men facing the wall, I attempted to shepherd her quickly to a stall. However, the row of men fascinated her.

"Why are they standing there?" she asked, in her naturally projecting voice.

"They have to pee," I replied matter-of-factly.

"On the *wall*?" she said in surprise.

We reached a stall, and I propelled her gently, but quickly inside, pulling the door closed behind us. She cast a curious eye about the enclosure, and then peered into the toilet bowl. Her frown informed me that all was not well.

"I can't use this potty."

"Why not?"

"There's sediment in the bowl."

"There's what?" (I couldn't believe my ears!)

"There's sediment; see it down there. I don't like this potty."

She turned quickly. Her mind was made up and she was heading for another stall! Picking up my briefcase and Amy's travel case, I opened the door slowly and looked out to see if the situation was clear and decent. Three feet below my eye level, another pair of eyes was peering from around my hips.

"Pappi, move! I've got to tinkle!"

A man, zipping up, threw a startled look at Amy. She ignored him as she walked resolutely to the next stall and pushed the door. It didn't budge.

"This door is stuck," she muttered, more to herself than to me.

She walked to the next stall, her Pappi close on her heels. A man came out and stared at her for a moment, bemused.

"Well, hello there...."

Amy brushed past him single-mindedly. "I have to tinkle." He looked at me, slightly annoyed.

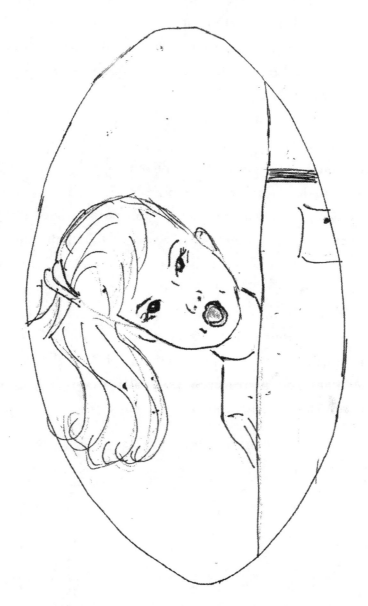

Three feet below my eye level, another pair of eyes was peering from around my hips.

"What's with Tinker-Bell?"

"I'm her grandfather. She's traveling with me."

"Hurry, Pappi. You've got to put toilet paper on the seat."

The man shook his head; he was not impressed with my explanation. "I can hardly take her into the women's rest room, can I?" I said after him, as he headed for the wash basins.

Turning again to Amy's needs, I grabbed the three yards of toilet paper which she was rapidly unrolling.

"You don't need so much," I said quickly.

"I need to tinkle," she replied firmly.

A moment later, balancing precariously on the tissue-lined horseshoe, Amy smiled up at me, a mixture of happy relief and simple trust in her eyes. My hands at her waist gave her a gentle squeeze.

"You really are a Tinkle-Bell," I said.

"I'm Tiffany-Amy," she stated emphatically.

As we were washing our hands, I looked at her pudgy little fingers. Our eldest daughter loved the name Tiffany; we loved the name Amy. No matter how you cut it, Tiffany-Amy was a well-loved little girl and she knew it. Her self-confidence showed that.

CHAPTER III

Weather Glitches

It was to be almost seven months before Amy and I were once more on our way for another trip. The day dawned pink and frosty, as only clear March mornings can. The family was excited driving to the Toronto Airport, with the exception of Amy's two year old little sister nicknamed "Furry". Furry wasn't going to Florida with us, and Furry wasn't pleased. I was busy reassuring her that when she was older, Pappi would take her on a trip, too. Clearly, she wasn't in the mood for reassurances that morning.

Furry was an affectionate nickname given to her by her mother a few days after she was born. Partly, it acknowledged the last syllable of her given name, Jennifer. Mostly, though, it was an irreverent reference to light-brown fuzz which covered her body when she was born. Within a few weeks of her birth, the fuzz disappeared; the nickname, however, remained.

By the time we reached the airport, the skies were overcast and it was raining lightly. We parked the car and made our way inside the terminal. Being an international flight, we had to go through U.S. Customs. Ever diligent to a variety of nefarious possibilities whenever a child is traveling alone with an adult male, the immigration officer pored over

Amy's birth certificate and other documents with considerable care. A buxom black lady, she peered down at my granddaughter.

"What's your name, child?"

"Tiffany-Amy."

"Who's this man here?"

"He's my Pappi. We're going to Florida to see Grammy!"

There was a period of silence as the officer looked over the documents again.

"Where do you live, Amy?"

(Unbeknown to the officer, my respect for her had just made a quantum leap. It was not just for her diligence, but also for knowing an Amy when she saw one.)

"I live at 421 Wood Park Drive," Amy replied quickly. She was obviously enjoying all the attention.

"Do you know your phone number, darlin'?"

"691-4182," Amy said, grinning with obvious pride. But the officer was still not satisfied.

"Why are you taking this child to Florida?" she asked me officiously.

"To see her grandmother," I replied, "like she said."

"You don't live with your wife?"

"We're getting a new office started down there. My wife is running it."

The officer smiled warmly at Amy, then cast another suspicious look at me. "How do I know if this letter giving permission for you to take Amy on a trip was *actually* written by her mother?"

"Her mother is right over there," I replied, pointing at my daughter Cara standing by the ticket counter, her face showing concern over our delay.

The officer waved Cara over. "Is this your daughter?"

"Yes."

"You two don't resemble her at all."

Cara replied quickly. "She's dark, like her father. He's Hispanic."

The officer frowned slightly, then went on. It was plain she had taken a fancy to Amy and wasn't going to take any chances. "Did you write this letter?"

"Yes."

"Do you know this lady, Amy?"

"She's my Mommy."

Cara pulled out her driver's license and handed it to the officer who examined it closely.

"Okay," the officer stated, handing everything back to us. "It looks like everything is in order. My apologies for the delay, and thank you." She turned to Amy with a big smile. "You have a wonderful time on the plane, Amy."

Amy vowed that she would, kissed her mother and Furry goodbye once more, then pulled on my hand. "We've got to get on the plane, Pappi. Come on!"

I waved goodbye to the officer, my daughter and Furry. The officer and Cara waved back, both smiling; a stoic Furry just stood and frowned. Amy pulled me through the X-ray check, then on towards the inner waiting area and the lunch stand - the one with doughnuts and apple juice. She obviously remembered that stand from the last trip we took together.

"I'm hungry," she said, a big smile of anticipation lighting-up her face. Despite her reputation as a picky eater, Amy was developing a taste for airport food, especially sweet stuff.

As we waited for the boarding call, the drizzly rain outside was being joined by a thickening fog. Heavy clouds were slowly but steadily dropping. A few minutes later, we were informed that our plane (inbound from Buffalo) was circling and looking for a window in the weather. The window wasn't found.

A soft female voice came over the loudspeaker: "We regret to announce that flight 476 to Pittsburgh has been cancelled. Passengers are requested to return to our ticket counter to arrange for alternate flights."

"Come on, Amy, we have to get our tickets changed."

"But, I want to go on the airplane."

"We have to take another one."

"Is the airplane broken, Pappi?"

"No. It's just late."

I was walking quickly now, with Amy holding tightly to my hand as she trotted beside me. "You're walking too fast, Pappi," she said.

"You're feet are too slow, Amy," I replied.

She looked up at me quizzically. I reduced my stride somewhat, but we still reached the ticket counter ahead of the crowd. The agent examined our tickets, tapped on her computer keyboard and gazed intently at the monitor. Amy, sitting on the counter, was fascinated.

"I can't look at that TV because I can't read."

"You can read it when you're older," I told her and kissed her cheek. She laughed.

The ticket agent apologized for the trouble, and explained that the earliest possible flight would be at 2:30 in the afternoon. That meant more than five hours of waiting with an active three and a half year old. I thanked him, took the tickets, and then called my mother who lived a few miles from the airport.

"Our flight has been delayed, Mum. How would you like a couple of visitors for a few hours?" My mother was delighted, but Amy was full of questions. She didn't understand why I was trying to find a cab and going to Nonna's house.* Clearly perturbed at the change in plans, she expressed her dissatisfaction pointedly. "If the plane can't fly, they should get another one!"

"They did. We will be on the other airplane in about five hours."

"That's too long, Pappi. I have no patience!"

The cab driver turned and looked at Amy admiringly. "You tell 'em, kid!"

---

* Italian for grandmother.

CHAPTER IV

Making Friends

When we arrived at my mother's home, I phoned Lili to explain the change in our flight departure. Amy wanted to talk to her Grammy, and rather sternly expressed her upset over the delay. Later, she didn't want to eat or sleep. So, she enjoyed television while Mum and I chatted over coffee about how things were going with the Tampa office. Amy soon became bored watching TV and asked me to give her a "drunken pony ride".

"What in the world is that?" Mum asked.

"Just watch," I replied, getting down on my hands and knees. "The grandchildren love it just as our girls did." Amy quickly climbed into the saddle.

As a "drunken-pony", I first lurched to the left then rocked to the right; I stumbled and staggered, shook and twisted. The challenge for any child on my back was to stay on, despite all the jerks and gyrations. Mum hooted hilariously watching Amy, who was holding on to my neck very tightly. Eventually, with a rapid rearing motion, I dumped her on the couch. Still eager for more, she then wanted a "footlift summersault", followed by a request for a "Pappi-pincher", and other similar physical play activities I had developed for our three daughters

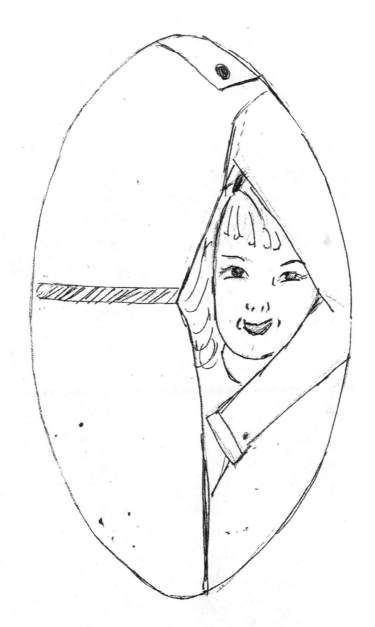

"Amy, child! What are you doing here?"

many years before. Although Amy showed no flagging of energy, mine was definitely giving out.

"How about a rest, Amy?"

As I sat down on an easy chair, Mum came over and gave me a hug. "This is what Dads and Pappis are for," she murmured. "This is what it's all about."

An hour and a half later, Amy and I were once again checking-in at the airport ticket counter. As we cleared U.S. Immigration for the second time that day, Amy (now familiar with the routine) started toward the inner lobby and the lunch stand. Suddenly, a familiar voice rang out: "Amy child! What are you doing here?"

Striding over to Amy was our friend the U.S. Immigration Officer, obviously on a break. Stopping Amy's headlong rush toward doughnuts and juice, the officer went down quickly on one knee - a protective arm around Amy's shoulders. "Where's your grandpa?" she demanded, very perturbed.

"Not far behind," I answered, walking up to them.

The officer got up, a look of amazement spreading across her face. "What happened?" she asked. "I thought you two were long gone."

I quickly explained what had happened, as she shook her head. Turning again to Amy, she bent over - her face all smiles; Amy entered her arms easily and gave her a big hug. Obviously pleased at Amy's spontaneous affection, the officer kissed her on the head. Waving again as we made our way towards the waiting area, she called-out to us.

"Have a good flight." She then added a postscript just for me: You take good care of my Amy, hear!"

"I will," I replied. "That's a promise." Hand-in-hand, Amy and I headed for the lunch stand.

As it turned out, that just wasn't our day! Unbelievably, the 2:30 p.m. flight was also cancelled. The problem (according to the unruffled female voice on the loudspeaker) was mechanical difficulties. Grabbing Amy by the shoulder, I once again started back towards the ticket counter. Amy, now somewhat jaded by the delays, looked up at me. With a hand on her hip, she asked: "Is the plane late again?"

"No. This time it is broken! We have to get another plane."

We walked deliberately to the ticket counter and I spoke to the same agent who had checked us in an hour earlier. She listened patiently as I described the series of events which repeatedly were delaying our departure for Florida. She said she would speak to her supervisor. "Can you come back in about fifteen minutes?" she asked.

I assured her that would be no problem and accompanied Amy to a nearby candy counter. After a quick perusal of the many delicious delights displayed there, she took a pass on the chocolate bars and decided instead upon a plastic box of Tic-Tacs. Those she could suck or chomp on, depending upon her level of patience.

"You can have two Tic-Tacs," I said. Amy promptly poured out four. Her eyes twinkled up at me as I closed the top and placed the candy box in her little Barbie travel case.

"The rest are for later, when we're on the plane...okay!" She nodded amiably in response.

A surprise awaited us when we got back to the ticket agent; she looked somewhat abashed as she spoke. "The only flight we can get you both on today is with another carrier, leaving Buffalo at 5:50 p.m. But, there are no connecting flights to Buffalo. So-o-o (My anxiety hung on her "o's"), we've decided to send you to the Buffalo Airport by limousine!"

"By limousine?"

"Yes. If you leave immediately, you should be able to make it. We have notified Buffalo that you are being re-routed."

Grasping the limousine voucher (and my briefcase) in one hand

and Amy in the other, I started towards the exit doors. She was holding her travel case tightly.

Where are we going, Pappi? Are we going on the other plane now?"

"We have to go to another airport, Amy. We'll catch the plane at the other airport."

The trip to Buffalo was only as uneventful as travel anywhere can be when traveling with an Amy. She kept up an almost uninterrupted conversation with our driver who seemed to enjoy the interchange as much as she did.

"Is it a long way to the other airport?"

"Yes, kiddo. It's a long way."

"Is it a *really* long way?"

"Yes, a really long way."

(Silence) Then: "How long is that?"

"Pretty far."

"Pretty far?"

"Like, a really, long far way."

"I think that's too far!"

It took a few moments of reassurances from the driver and me to convince Amy that "long far away" wasn't actually too far. By that time, after few more Tic-Tacs, the control panel of electric switches on the arm rest had shifted Amy's focus. Delightedly, as we sped on our way toward the U.S. border, she flicked the two rear-seat lights off and on until I distracted her.

After about an hour on the road, Amy de-activated somewhat. Looking a bit sleepy, she leaned over and placed her head on my lap. (Those were the days before stringent seat-belt restrictions.) It was 4:20 p.m. in the afternoon and she had been on the go since six thirty in the morning. A good nap was just what she needed. I stroked her head and pony-tail, and then slipped my fingers softly across her cheek.

Wrong move! She sat bolt-upright on the seat and stated emphatically: "I'm not sleepy!" Then, "I love you, Pappi". She gave me a big hug and kissed me soundly on the cheek.

"What about me, Amy?" The driver was smiling back at her through his rear-view mirror.

"I don't love you, yet. Maybe later." The driver broke up.

"Why is he laughing, Pappi?"

"He thinks you're funny."

That struck Amy as amusing, and she began to laugh too. She stood on the floor hump and peered over the back of the seat at the driver.

"My sister Furry is funny, but I'm more funny."

"Well, she has a funny name. Do you have a funny name, too? Like a nickname?"

"What's a nickname?"

"A special fun-name, one that only your family and friends call you."

Amy became suddenly serious. She turned to look at me, her dark eyes searching mine.

"Do I have one of those?"

"A nickname?"

"Yes. Do I have a nickname, Pappi?"

"Well, I called you Tinkle Bell once."

That settled the issue very quickly. "I'm not Tinkle Bell. I'm Tiffany-Amy."

"Well, maybe Amy is your nickname. For Grammy and me it's your special name."

She turned again to the driver and announced proudly: "My nickname is Amy."

"Amy," he repeated thoughtfully. "I like it! That's a good nickname."

Amy leaned forward on her tip-toes, stretching toward the driver. He smiled at her in the rear-view mirror, genuinely pleased with the neck hug she bestowed.

A little while later, we arrived at the U.S. border. The Immigration Officer at the booth peered inquisitively back at us as he questioned the driver. "Where are you headed?"

"Buffalo International," the driver replied. "These folks have to catch a flight there."

"Where are you coming from?"

"Toronto."

"Kind of a round-about way to catch a plane, isn't it?"

Not waiting for the driver to answer, the officer turned his attention to us. Putting down the window, I handed him my copy of the voucher, our flight tickets and Amy's documentation. He scrutinized everything closely, and then turned to Amy. "Where are you going, young lady?"

"We're going to another airport. Our plane was broken." (I began to explain further, but the officer waved me off.)

"Who's that man, sweetheart?" (He pointed at me with a sturdy index finger.)

"That's my Pappi."

"And who are you?"

"I'm Tiffany-Amy."

"Where are you going on the plane?"

"To see my Grammy."

The officer looked at me again. "Are you her grandfather?"

"Yes. I'm taking her to see her grandmother in Florida."

"You're divorced?"

"No, it's a business thing. My wife administers a new office for us there. You have the letter from my daughter giving me permission to take Amy to Florida."

He pulled out the letter and read it quickly. After about seven minutes at the border, the officer was still checking our documentation. We only had twenty five minutes to get to the airport, a piece of information offered by the driver which may have cut short the officer's inquiry. At any rate, he handed back our tickets and documents, nodded - and allowed us to pass. (Although we were in a hurry, I felt very reassured by the careful attention which the U.S. Immigration Officers give to small children crossing the border.)

Our limousine sped down the highway. Taking the Airport cut-off abruptly, the driver guided the big Lincoln skillfully through the late afternoon traffic. With only ten minutes to spare, he pulled up at the terminal building. He handed me my suitcase and wished us a good flight. I handed him a tip, Amy waved goodbye, then she and I ran inside.

We rushed up to the ticket counter. The young woman glanced quickly at our tickets and prepared our boarding passes.

"Glad to see you guys made it," she laughed.

"Me, too - and thanks for everything."

Ten minutes later, we were in the air and headed for Charlotte, North Carolina, the first leg of our flight to Tampa. It had been quite a day, but we were finally on our way.

CHAPTER V

Chica-Chica

Amy has an amazing memory and a one-track mind. We were hardly in the air before she was reaching for her Tic-Tacs.

"Remember, Amy, only two at a time."

She remembered and this time dutifully tipped out just two of the small, white candies. She put them in her mouth, and clipped the lid shut on the small plastic box.

Then, the rhythm sequence began. Amy was holding her box of Tic-Tacs tightly in her left hand and shaking it in jerky syncopated movements.

Chica-chica, Chica-chica, chica-chica, chica-chica!

"Be careful, Amy! The top could flip open!"

I placed her left thumb firmly on the lid; once more she began shaking her syncopated beat.

After a few more minutes with her musical mints, Amy decided it was time to stand up on her seat and look around. She quickly got into a discussion with an attractive young university coed seated behind us.

"I'm going to see Grammy in Florida." (I loved the way she accented the second syllable, Flor-E-da.)

"That's wonderful. I'm going to Florida, too."

Chica-chica, chica-chica, chica-chica - -

"My name is Tiffany-Amy."

"Really? That's great. *My* name is Amy, too."

"Pappi! Her name is Amy, just like my name!"

She was incredulous at this discovery. Then she brightened. "I think I love her!"

Little Amy was absolutely enchanted with her new-found friend. They were soon chatting amiably as we sped across the skies.

"I have a little sister," Amy proclaimed proudly.

"What's her name?" her new friend asked.

"Furry"

"My, that's an unusual name, isn't it?"

"Her real name is Jennifer."

"Jennifer. That's really cute! Jennifer Furry."

"Do you know what Furry does?"

"No, sweetheart, what does Furry do?"

"She picks her nose."

"Oh!" Our coed went suddenly quiet.

"And you know what else? Sometimes her nose bleeds!"

There was a decided lack of response from behind us. I was very grateful that meals weren't being served. I leaned over and got Amy interested in her coloring book. "Sit down now, sweetheart. Do a nice picture for Pappi."

Amy settled down on the seat, glanced briefly at the clouds outside the window, then began thumbing through the pages of her Barbie-Doll coloring book.

"Can I have some Tic-Tacs?"

"Yes. How many can you have?"

"Two."

"That's right."

Before long, Amy was deeply engaged in the creative arts. With her right hand, she was being careful to stay within the lines; with her left hand she was once more beating out a rhythm.

Chick-chicka, chick-chick-chicka - -

She hummed happily as she sucked on her Tic-Tacs. Amy was contented, I was drowsy - and all was well with the world. I leaned back in my seat, sighed and closed my eyes.

"Oh! My Tic-Tacs!"

Amy's squeal of alarm jolted me. I opened my eyes just in time to see a shower of Tic-Tacs fly onto the seat and my lap.

"Amy! Didn't Pappi tell you to keep your thumb on the lid?"

Having forewarned her earlier, I was quite irritated. With someone as sensitive as Amy, that meant tears. The big silent drops flopped over her eye-lashes and dribbled down her cheeks.

"It's okay, Amy," I said quickly. "You still have a few left in the box."

She sniffed a bit, stopped crying, and then jumped to the floor. Picking up the Tic-Tacs from the seat, we dropped them carefully into an air-sick bag.

Amy then shifted her search to my lap. She picked up a few more and placed them in the bag as well.

"Lift up your leg, Pappi!"

"What?"

"There's one under your leg!"

Amy's strident voice carried easily to those seated nearby. All conversation around us suddenly ceased. I lifted my leg.

"You see, Amy. There aren't any more."

"Yes, Pappi, there is! It must have slipped under your penis!" Her tone of indignation was exceeded only by my mortification.

Accompanied by muffled giggles from some of the closer passengers, I stood up. Amy pounced on a lonely Tic-Tac. Grasping it proudly, she

The big, silent drops flopped over her eyelashes...

dropped it into the bag. "That's the last one," she stated emphatically. Finally satisfied, she sat down once again, picked up her coloring book and withdrew into artistic concentration. As for me, I withdrew as far as I could into my seat.

Suddenly. "Can I have some more Tic-Tacs, Pappi?"

"Yes, Amy. Help yourself, but PLEASE don't shake the box!"

Our plane's stop-over in Charlotte turned out to be much longer than expected due to poor weather conditions. We located some seats in the Waiting Area, but it wasn't long before Amy became fidgety.

"Do you want to see my exercises, Pappi?"

She had been enrolled for a few weeks in a junior gymnastics class for preschoolers and was eager to demonstrate some of the routines she had learned.

"Sure," I said. "Show me your exercises."

For the next 20 minutes, encouraged by laughter from other waiting passengers, Amy performed knee-bends, abbreviated push-ups, pirouettes along with several other combinations and routines. She was an unmitigated hit. After awhile, she darted under the seats and enjoyed a delightful game of peek-a-boo with most, though not all, the waiting passengers. It was now after 9:00 p.m. and some of them were feeling too tired for games. Amazingly, though, Amy was still going strong. I suggested a nap, which only produced a determined shake of her head. Taking a nap was definitely not on her agenda.

"Pappi. I'm hungry." Those three words jogged my memory. She had eaten a muffin on the plane, but that had been two and a half hours earlier. And, Tic-Tacs do not a meal make!

"Okay, Amy. Let's get a hot-dog and some fries."

We walked to a nearby restaurant. Correction: I walked; Amy skipped, jumped and sashayed, her ponytail swinging merrily.

Once inside the restaurant, we sat at a small table. Amy was soon fascinated by two little girls who were seated with their mother in a near-by booth. We couldn't help overhearing their conversation as we ate. Unlike Amy, the two sisters were obviously very tired.

"Mommy! Cindy's squeezing me! Stop it, Cindy!"

"Cindy, stop squeezing your sister!"

"She's still squeezing me. Make her stop squeezing me!"

"Cindy! I asked you to stop squeezing your sister!"

"But I love her."

"Your sister just loves you, Jackie. You should be glad that she loves you."

"I don't want her to love me right now."

"Cindy, stop loving your sister."

"When *can* I love her?"

"I don't know. Maybe later."

"When, later?"

"I don't know. Ask your sister."

"When can I love you, Cindy?"

"Never."

"Mommy-y-y-y!"

Amy's reaction to the whole scenario was typical. "When I want to love Furry, she gets hugged!"

Later, aloft once again, our flight to Tampa was uneventful. Amy spent much of the next hour and a half hanging over the back of the seat, chatting and playing hand games with coed Amy. I took the opportunity to grab a few winks. Maybe Amy wasn't tired, but her Pappi was definitely feeling the effects of the long day.

While in Charlotte, I had phoned my wife to explain that we had been delayed and were on another flight which had been diverted to St. Petersburg, the small airport south of Tampa. Lili said she would be there. As our plane began its slow descent, I found myself thinking

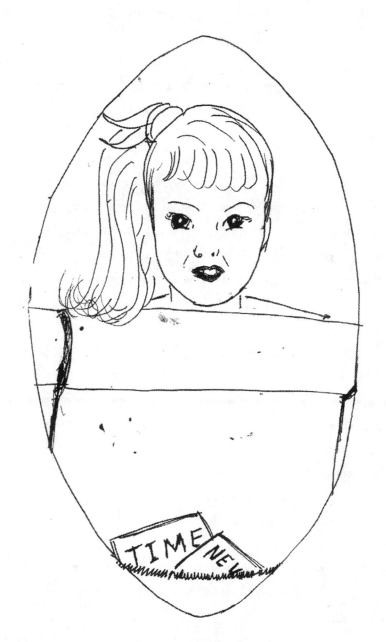

Amy spent much of the trip...

warmly of Lili. It had been a long day for her too, and here it was, practically midnight, and we were just arriving. As the plane taxied up to the tarmac and the jet motors whined down, Amy unbuckled herself and jumped down off the seat. She had decided that she wanted to leave the plane with her new friend Amy, who gladly took her hand. They went down the aisle with the slowly-exiting throng. I took down my briefcase and Amy's travel case, and joined the exodus.

Deplaning in St. Petersburg meant a walk across the tarmac to the terminal building. I remember thinking how like the 1950s the whole set-up was; there was no convenient enclosed ramp here. Up ahead, our Amy was bobbing along happily with coed Amy. Suddenly, little Amy caught sight of her grandmother standing at the large glass doors.

"Grammy! Grammy!" With arms outstretched she dashed forward, leaving her new friend behind. Catching up to the young lady, we traded smiles.

"Fickle, ain't she?!" I commented with a chuckle.

"She sure loves her Grandmother," Amy responded good-naturedly.

"Absolutely! When her Grammy is around, everyone else plays second fiddle."

Lili met us, with Amy in her arms.

"Lili," I said. "Meet another Amy."

We all walked along, chatting and laughing. After the two Amys hugged each other goodbye, I suggested that Lili go ahead and wait by the entrance while I claimed my suitcase. Ten minutes later, I walked up to the bench where Lili and our Amy were sitting. Lili got up as I approached.

"What went on during that flight?" she asked, her eyebrows arched curiously.

"What do you mean?"

"Well, many of the passengers leaving the terminal seemed to know Amy by name. They were laughing and waving goodbye to her. What happened?"

"It's a long story," I said. "I'll tell you about it on the way home."

As Lili drove out of the airport parking lot, I looked at Amy in the back seat. She was sprawled across the blanket, totally zonked by fatigue. The long day had finally caught up with her. Turning onto the highway, Lili yawned. I glanced at my watch.

"Wow! It's quarter to one in the morning." I gave Lili's arm an affectionate squeeze and she gave me a quick shoulder-snuggle.

"We've got one amazing little granddaughter," I sighed.

"That's our Amy," Lili replied

CHAPTER VI

At TheBeach

During Amy's first trip with me to Florida, we didn't have the opportunity to take her to the beach. On this second trip, my wife and I were determined to give her a day with the sand and the sea. So, around 10 a.m. on a typical warm and clear day, we put the top down on Lili's classic 1968 Skylark Convertible and headed for the beach. Amy was delighted, preening proudly in her new swimsuit. It was a wildly colorful purple and chartreuse number that could have been easily seen from low-flying space craft. She wasn't going to get lost while she was with us.

As we drove slowly along the beach road searching for a parking spot, Amy pointed excitedly at the water: "Look, Grammy! Lake Ontario."

We laughed, and my wife explained. "You're not in Ontario now, sweetheart. That's the Gulf of Mexico."

"It's not Lake Ontario?"

"No, it's the Gulf of Mexico. Can you say that?"

Amy was locked into deep concentration as I parked the car. Her mouth moved slowly over the words.

"The...Gulf...of...."

"Mexico," my wife repeated.

'The Gulf of ... Mex-i-co."

"That's right! She said it perfectly, Pappi."

"Good for you, Amy."

"The Gulf of Mexico, the Gulf of Mexico," Amy repeated the words happily. It was another acquisition by that eager young mind.

As Lili and I spread the blanket on the sand, Amy ran for the water. Gentle waves were rolling-in along the shore and she delighted in jumping over them. We watched with considerable pleasure as she stomped her feet in a splashy march through the shallows while searching for seashells. Then, unexpectedly, a slightly larger wave hit her across the chest and knocked her backwards onto her bottom. She howled in fright.

Lili and I ran to pick her up. Standing Amy on her feet, we reassured her that she was going to be just fine. Sobbing, she tried to speak through her tears.

"The Gulf of Mexico...it...it...slapped me right in the face!"

Lili and I started to laugh, but Amy was not amused. She didn't like being laughed at and a disapproving pout came over her face. "It's not very funny, you know," she said indignantly.

Stifling her laughter, Lili wrapped her arms around Amy and soothed her. "That wasn't very nice of the Gulf of Mexico. But, I don't think it will happen again."

A few minutes later, Amy was chasing me through the surf; her indignation and upset quickly forgotten. All-in-all, the three of us had a wonderful time at the beach that day.

Our granddaughter's inventiveness never stopped. Later, after dinner, as we were eating dessert, Amy instinctively shoved pieces of chocolate cake onto her fork. Noticing the smudged frosting on her fingers, I handed her a napkin. She paid no attention to it.

"Aren't you going to wipe off your fingers, Amy?"

"I did…in here." She pointed to her chocolate encrusted mouth.

So much for the niceties of etiquette! Before I could suggest that she wipe off her mouth, her tongue was busy picking up all stray traces of chocolate on her lips and chin. She was not one to waste good chocolate frosting on a napkin.

CHAPTER VII

Twins

Nine days later, on our way back to Toronto, we had a one hour stop-over in Philadelphia. Sitting in the Waiting Area, Amy was amazed at her first sight of twins. The two little sisters, about four years of age, seemed to be playing some form of musical chairs without any music; they were leaping on and off the seats. Amy was reluctant to join-in, but watched them intently.

"Those are identical twins, Amy."

"What are twins?"

"Little sisters born almost at the same time and look the same."

"Do they have the same birthday?"

"Yes, they do."

There was a long pause as Amy looked at them playing.

"Do they have the same name, Pappi?"

"No. Each one has her own name."

"Well, that's good!"

Just then, the two little girls ran over to where we were seated by the windows. They climbed up on the seats and looked at the airplanes parked outside.

"Look," one of them said suddenly. "Twin planes."

I turned. Two identical jet-liners were facing us, side-by-side.

"Are they really twins?" the other sister asked.

"Yes."

"Are they girl or boy planes?"

"I can't tell until they turn around," the obviously wiser sister replied gravely, "like Mommy did with our kittens."

When they jumped back onto the floor, the twins looked at Amy for a moment before walking back to their mother who was seated nearby. Amy sat quietly and continued to watch them closely. Then, she leaned toward me and whispered.

"I'm glad Furry has her own face," she commented thoughtfully.

EPILOG

Mark Twain once noted with reference to Tom Sawyer, that anyone writing about children must be aware when a specific age-period is coming to an end. Just as Twain noted that Tom's boyhood was just about over, I also must now point out that Amy is long past being a preschooler. My travels with her came to an end when she started kindergarten and was no longer as free to travel. The days were well behind us when it was possible for Amy to just pick-up and leave with me on one of my business trips to Tampa. She is now a college graduate with many new and different responsibilities. As for me, I'm retired.

How fast the years have passed, and how quickly Amy grew into adulthood. It is sobering to realize how rapidly her childhood passed. Those pudgy little fingers are long and slender now; her face has gracefully matured into that of a lovely young woman. She has changed in other ways as well, being less likely now to charge forward eagerly into each new experience as she once did. During her teen years, our Amy became more conscious of her peer group and learned to check out carefully what the other kids were doing before saying: "I can do that!"

Along with a heightened consciousness of her peers, Lili and I have noticed a recently discovered self-consciousness. The former was inevitable; the latter, hopefully, will not hinder the spontaneity and affectionate trusting which was so much a part of her personality as a child.

My travels with Amy were an unexpected and marvelous opportunity to closely experience one of our grandchildren in a variety of amusing circumstances. Her use of language, along with an infectious laugh, was more delightful to her Grammy and Pappi than she will ever realize. A few of those experiences, as chronicled here, have been penned as a loving memento for Amy in years yet to be. They are also offered as a genuine thank you to her, along with deep appreciation to her mother, father and sister, for making possible such an amusing traveling companion during those wonderful days of yesteryear.

Mario Bartoletti
2008

Printed in the United States
By Bookmasters